THE BALLAD OF US

A POETIC ODE TO LOVE'S MANY FORMS

AKANKSHA BISHT

Copyright © Akanksha Bisht
All Rights Reserved.

This book has been self-published with all reasonable efforts taken to make the material error-free by the author. No part of this book shall be used, reproduced in any manner whatsoever without written permission from the author, except in the case of brief quotations embodied in critical articles and reviews.

The Author of this book is solely responsible and liable for its content including but not limited to the views, representations, descriptions, statements, information, opinions and references ["Content"]. The Content of this book shall not constitute or be construed or deemed to reflect the opinion or expression of the Publisher or Editor. Neither the Publisher nor Editor endorse or approve the Content of this book or guarantee the reliability, accuracy or completeness of the Content published herein and do not make any representations or warranties of any kind, express or implied, including but not limited to the implied warranties of merchantability, fitness for a particular purpose. The Publisher and Editor shall not be liable whatsoever for any errors, omissions, whether such errors or omissions result from negligence, accident, or any other cause or claims for loss or damages of any kind, including without limitation, indirect or consequential loss or damage arising out of use, inability to use, or about the reliability, accuracy or sufficiency of the information contained in this book.

Made with ♥ on the Notion Press Platform
www.notionpress.com

To the poets and writers who have shown me the power the words.

Contents

Foreword — *vii*

Preface — *ix*

Acknowledgements — *xi*

1. Fated Encounter — 1
2. The Paper Trail Of Love — 3
3. Spring's Renewal — 5
4. Symphony Of Love — 7
5. Intertwined — 9
6. Are You Feeling It Too? — 11
7. Fireflies — 13
8. Wildfire Hearts — 14
9. A Dance For Two — 16
10. What Is Love, You Say? — 17
11. Under The Same Sky — 19
12. Stolen Moments — 20
13. Endless — 22
14. Burning Desires — 24
15. A Summer Dream — 26
16. Veiled Love — 28
17. "all Yours" — 30
18. Fragments Of Us — 32
19. Heartstrings — 34
20. Echoes Of Euphoria — 36

End Note — 39

Foreword

Love is a journey, an adventure that takes us through a maze of emotions and experiences, leaving behind memories that we cherish forever. "The Ballad of Us" is a collection of poetry that explores the beautiful, complex, and often unpredictable nature of love.

In these pages, you will find a symphony of love, a melody that plays in the hearts of two people deeply connected. The words will take you on a journey through the ups and downs of relationships, the joy and the pain of falling in love, and the beauty of being lost in the moment.

The poems in this collection are like fragments of a beautiful mosaic, each piece adding to the overall picture of the story of love. From the eternal flames of passion to the fragility of stolen moments, each poem offers a glimpse into the heart of the author.

As you read through "The Ballad of Us," you will find yourself entwined in the words, lost in the firefly dreams of two hearts that beat as one. You will dance with the couple in a delicate waltz for two and follow the paper trail of their love story. You will feel the sweet intoxication of love and the tangle of emotions that comes with it.

FOREWORD

This collection is a reminder that love is universal, it transcends time and space, and it is the glue that holds us together. So, sit back, relax, and let the words wash over you. Let the echoes of euphoria linger, and the fragments of us stay with you long after the last page is turned.

With "The Ballad of Us," I invite you to join me on a journey through the many faces of love and to experience the beauty and power of this incredible force that binds us all.

Sincerely,
Akanksha Bisht

Preface

This collection of poems celebrates the beauty and power of human connection.
Through vivid imagery and heartfelt emotion, these poems explore the many facets of love, from the tender moments shared between two souls to the fiery passion that ignites between them.

Acknowledgements

I would like to express my deepest gratitude to my parents, who have always been a pillar of support in all my endeavors, including this book. Without their love, encouragement, and unwavering support, this project would not have been possible.

With heartfelt gratitude, I express my deep appreciation to my dear friend Rohit, who has provided unwavering guidance, support, and praise, always offering his presence and unconditional acceptance regardless of my decisions.

My heartfelt thanks go to my school teachers especially, my English and Hindi teachers whose love for the language and literature inspired me to pursue my passion for writing.

Finally, I would like to extend my sincere thanks to all the readers who have taken the time to read this book. I hope that these poems have touched your hearts and kindled within you the same emotions that inspired me to write them.

1. Fated encounter

At eighteen, I saw you from afar,
At a friend's party, chatting with the stars,
I caught a glimpse, a mere fleeting view,
But something within me just knew.

The night progressed, with turns of my mind,
In my subconscious, thoughts intertwined,
You approached, and asked to be friends,
A connection sparked, with no foreseeable ends.

We were from different cities, miles apart,
But through late-night calls, we shared our hearts,
As our friendship blossomed, so did my concealed desire,
A sensation that burned like an unquenchable fire.

We laughed and smiled, our bond ever so strong,
But beneath the surface, I knew I didn't belong,
For every moment with you, my heart grew fonder,
But I dared not say it, afraid to ponder.
Our tale unfolded, like a dream in the night,
But like a flickering flame, it struggled to ignite,
We were two young souls, with hidden feelings inside,
With no clue what was evolving, like a rose in disguise.

We talked and we laughed, as friends we would be,
But beneath the surface, something we couldn't see,
Like a river that flows, deep and unseen,
A tale began, with a mystery in between.

2. The paper trail of love

Reveal a story untold,
A love that burned within his soul,
A passion he dared not show,
And so he wrote, in words so bold,
All the feelings he could not withhold.

The crumpled papers bore witness true,
To a heart that longed for someone new,
A heart that beat with love so pure,
A heart that sought to find a cure.

For the pain that lingered deep inside,
The pain that could no longer hide,
The pain that kept him up all night,
The pain that refused to take flight.

And so he poured his heart out in ink,
On those crumpled papers that lay in a heap,
Hoping that someday she would see,
The love that he had kept so deep.

But fate had other plans in store,
And his love remained forevermore,

Lost in the pages of his life,
Forgotten, but never out of sight.

For his love was real, and it was true,
And though he never said,
she always knew,
In her heart, his memory lived on,
A love that burned bright,
long after he was gone.

And so the crumpled papers lay,
A testament to love,
in every way,
A story untold, yet still so true,
A love that will forever be,
just between the two.

3. Spring's renewal

You entered my life like a blooming spring,
A canvas of colors and scents so sweet,
A newfound joy, a song I yearned to sing,
A new beginning, a fresh heartbeat.

You were the rain that quenched my parched soul,
A fountain of youth, a soothing balm,
A warm embrace that made me feel whole,
A ray of sunshine in life's storm.

With your arrival, I bloomed like a flower,
And your love nourished me like the earth,
You brought me peace and gave me power,
And in you, I found my heart's worth.

You are the spring of my life,
my guiding light,
The one that brings renewal and hope,
A warm fire on a cold winter's night,
A safe haven where I can cope.

You came into my life like a spring so true,
A season of change, a time to renew,

And with every passing day,
I'm grateful for you,
My heart's eternal spring, forever new.

4. Symphony of love

You're the beat in my heart,
the air that I breathe,
My soulmate, my forever,
the one I'll never leave.
My love, you were meant to be mine,
As much a part of me as the stars that shine.

Oh, my love, you are the death of me,
But in your arms, I am free.
We'll stand the test of time,
Together, forever, you'll always be mine.

In the early light of day,
when the world is still asleep,
We'll hold each other close,
our love we'll always keep.
As the sun rises high, our love will grow,
Stronger and deeper, with each passing blow.

Oh, my love, you are the death of me,
But in your arms, I am free.
We'll stand the test of time,
Together, forever, you'll always be mine.

Through the ups and the downs,
the joy and the pain,
Our love will endure, never to wane.
We'll weather the storms and dance in the rain,
Together we'll conquer, our love will remain.

Oh, my love, you are the death of me,
But in your arms, I am free.
We'll stand the test of time,
Together, forever, you'll always be mine.

You are mine, meant to be mine,
My love, my life, my everything divine.
Through the highs and the lows,
we'll always shine,
Together, forever, till the end of time.

5. Intertwined

Oh, my silly boy,
I love the way you lost and stayed,
Holding me tight, walking by my side
Through every season, every shade.

Our love grows more intense and glorious,
With every moment, every chance we get.
How much I love you?
Let me count the ways,
As thoughts of you invade my mind and set.

With illusions of our own paradise,
We cherished each other without compromise.
But now, the leaves have withered and fallen,
Impatient with the longing that has swollen.

Every day, every hour, every minute goes by,
Only to find dry flowers all around.
A dense storm whips the twiglets of October,
As autumn whispers with its whistling sound.

Our love will stay alive in my heart and soul,
Even as the distance between us takes its toll.

For every moment we shared, every kiss and touch,
Is etched in my memory, and I love you so much.
And though we may be apart for a while,
I know our love will never be exiled.
For it's stronger than any distance or time,
A bond that will endure and always shine.

So hold me close, my love, and never let go,
As we navigate life's unpredictable flow.
With you as my rock, I can brave any storm,
Our love a shelter, safe and warm.
Side by side, we'll weather the gales,
Our bond unbreakable, as firm as cliffs and trails.

Oh, my silly boy,
You are my everything, my joy.
I love you more with each passing day,
And in my heart, you'll forever stay.

6. Are you feeling it too?

In your arms, I am consumed
My heart aflame, with love entombed
Do you feel the fire, burning bright?
Can you sense the heat, in the dead of night?

With every touch, my passion grows
As the embers of desire, fiercely glows
Do you see the flames, in my eyes?
Can you feel the inferno, rise and rise?

Our bodies merge, in a blazing embrace
As the heat intensifies, with each loving trace
Do you hear the crackle, of the burning flame?
Can you taste the sweetness, of our love's game?

In the heat of our passion, we are undone
Our souls entwined, as we become one
Do you feel the heat, of our fiery bond?
Can you sense the love, that we have spawned?

Our love, like a wildfire, never fades
As we bask, in each other's loving shades
Do you feel the warmth, of our lasting fire?

Can you see the beauty, of our heart's desire?

7. Fireflies

I was chasing fireflies on a summer night,
Captivated by their glow, my heart alight.
With every step I took, they flew away,
Dancing out of reach, but I couldn't stay away.

And then I saw you, in the distance so bright,
A firefly of your own, your love a guiding light.
I chased after you, like I did with the bugs,
As I stumbled and fell, with heart full of tugs.

But you held out your hand, and lifted me up,
Your touch like magic, that filled my empty cup.
With you by my side, I felt alive and free,
As we chased our fireflies, a beautiful sight to see.

8. Wildfire hearts

Our love is like a wildfire
Burning bright, never to tire
Spreading fast and uncontrolled
Never to be contained or consoled

Madly in love, we burn together
Our passion like flames, hotter than ever
Nothing can put out this raging fire
Our love will blaze on, taking us higher

Our hearts like embers, glowing bright
Our souls intertwined, shining like light
Like a wildfire, we consume everything
But we're not burning out, we're just beginning

Madly in love, we burn together
Our passion like flames, hotter than ever
Nothing can put out this raging fire
Our love will blaze on, taking us higher

Our love like a forest on fire
Burning down walls, taking us higher
Embraced by flames, we are one

Ablaze with love, our journey's just begun

Madly in love, we burn together
Our passion like flames, hotter than ever
Nothing can put out this raging fire
Our love will blaze on, taking us higher.

9. A dance for two

In your embrace, I feel a melody,
A rhythm that resonates through me,
A dance that moves my every bone,
A song that makes my heart its home.

With every step, our feet align,
Our bodies move in perfect time,
We sway and spin in sweet embrace,
Our love a ballad, full of grace.

Each note a kiss, each beat a touch,
We weave our love into the rush,
Of passion, of desire, of pure bliss,
A symphony of love, sealed with a kiss.

Our love, a melody that sings,
A song that forever brings,
A rhythm that we dance along,
In perfect harmony, we belong.

10. What is love, you say?

What is love, you say?
It's in the way a face turns red
When caught in a moment of admiration unsaid,
And in the white that follows it;
The fluttering eyelids that can't seem to quit;
The smile that betrays the pain beneath it—
This is love, I say.

What is love, you say?
It's in the racing heartbeats, in the fray
Of emotions that leave us still and sore,
As new feelings make their way to the core,
Running through our veins like the morning sun,
As swift as its light, and its power undone—
This is love, I say.

What is love, you say?
It's in the distance we keep, the things we don't say,
The sudden silence, the tears we try to hide,
The joy that masks itself with fear inside,
As our hearts leap in the chest,
And we know, and we name, our heavenly guest—
This is love, I say.

What is love, you say?
It's in the pride that makes the haughty heart obey,
In the unnamed light that floods the world with grace,
In the resemblance of beauty to one cherished face,
In the gentle touch of trembling hands,
In the eyes and lips that reveal all of love's demands—
This is love, I say.

What is love, you say?
It's in the words that are timidly sent on their way,
The flashes of fire that light up a gaze,
Like the lightning that precedes the stormy days,
In the stillness that fills the soul,
In the warmth that makes our passions whole,
In the madness that dissolves in a sweet embrace,
And in the blissful frenzy of a lover's chase—
This is love, I say.

11. Under the same sky

Under the same sky, you and I lie
As our fingers weave, like a lullaby
The fragrance of life fills the air
And all our worries, we willingly share

The song of birds is a symphony
As we look up in perfect harmony
Your touch is like a soothing melody
And my heart is at peace, completely

This moment with you, is a moment of bliss
As we forget everything, in this kiss
Beneath the vast and infinite blue
My heart beats for no one else but you.

12. Stolen moments

Reminiscing the kisses I stole,
While you were deep in sleep,
I felt my heart skip, my body whole,
As I watched you dream so deep.

Your peaceful breaths, a soothing balm,
That put my anxious mind at rest,
In the quiet of the night, no harm,
As I kissed your lips, so blessed.

My fingers traced the lines of your face,
As I savoured each moment of delight,
And felt my heart's steady pace,
As I held you close, so tight.

Those moments were a precious gift,
A memory to keep close to my heart,
As I lay beside you, my spirits lift,
And I knew we would never be apart.

For in your arms, I found my home,
In your embrace, I found my truth,
And though the years may come and roam,

Our love will never lose its youth.

13. Endless

On the day when the sun forgets to shine,
And the wind loses its gentle caress,
The flowers and trees will bow in decline,
As nature mourns in deep distress.

The sky will fade into a veil of grey,
And the clouds will dry up their tears,
Rivers will run low, with nothing to say,
As the earth crumbles in its fears.

But in the stillness of this lifeless scene,
I find solace in your embrace,
For your love is a light, forever gleaming,
A beacon of hope in this desolate space.

We are the fire that refuses to die,
A tree that never surrenders its fight,
Our love is a river that never runs dry,
And a sky that forever glows in light.

So before all of this comes to pass,
Let us savour each moment, yours and mine,
For our love is a flame that will forever last,

In this world, and beyond, until the end of time.

14. Burning desires

It starts with a spark, a flicker in the night
A flame that ignites, setting the world alight
With each breath, the fire grows stronger
Our desire, like an inferno, lasts longer

Our passion, a wildfire, burning bright
Guiding us through the darkest night
The little things, the fuel that we need
To keep our desires, burning with heed

The tender whispers, like a soft breeze
The stolen glances, like a river that flees
Our hearts, like two magnets, drawn together
A force that defies, the toughest weather

Together, we're a blazing trail
Our desires, an unyielding sail
For our flame, shines through the night
Leading us through, the darkest plight
So let our fire, rage like a storm

For in each other's eyes, we transform
And in our burning desires, we find

A love that's forever, unconfined.

"I could feel you, burning inside of me," he whispered, his hand on her cheek.
"I could feel you too, like the beating of my heart," she replied, her eyes shining with tears.
"I am who I am because of you," he said, his voice choked with emotion.
"And I'll be who I'll be because of you," she replied, smiling through her tears.

15. A summer dream

In the depths of my heart, a garden blooms,
With flowers that yearn for a love that consumes.
Their petals open wide, reaching for the sun,
Desperate for warmth, for a love that has just begun.

But time moves slowly, and the sun sets in the sky,
Leaving the garden in darkness, and my heart to cry.
It longs for a love that's strong, one that won't fade,
A love that won't wither, or be lost in the shade.

Like a river that flows, my heart longs to be free,
To be carried away by the current, to a love that's meant to be.
But the waters are still, and my heart is still waiting,
Hoping for a love that will leave it no longer aching.

In my mind's eye, I see a bird in flight,
Soaring high above, free from the night.
Its wings carry it far, to a place of peace,
Where love is waiting, and heartache will cease.

My heart longs for that flight, to soar up high,
To be carried by love, and never to say goodbye.
To find a love that's true, like the bird in the sky,

A love that will carry me, until the day I die.

So, I wait in the garden, with flowers that yearn,
Hoping for a love that will return.
My heart is patient, my heart is strong,
For a love that will last, my whole life long.

16. Veiled love

In a quiet corner of the museum,
Behind the velvet rope,
Lies a painting of a love so hidden,
Only the brushstrokes can elope.

Two figures, intertwined in embrace,
Their love forbidden, their passion ablaze,
The artist captured every detail and trace,
Of their love, hidden in plain sight, for days.

The way his hand holds her waist so tight,
The way her eyes shine, reflecting the light,
Their love so pure, yet hidden from sight,
Their stolen moments, a secret delight.
As I stand here, staring at the canvas,
My heart aching with the beauty so grand,
I can't help but wonder, in a love so heinous,
What did they do, to keep love's flame fanned?

Did they steal kisses, in the dead of night,
Did they whisper sweet nothings, under the moonlight,
Did they dream of a future, bright and light,
Even though their love was hidden from sight?

Oh, hidden love, so sweet and pure,
Your passion and devotion, forever endure,
Will you remain hidden, forever obscure?
Or will you rise and shine, like the stars, forevermore?

17. "All yours"

Listening to that song takes me back in time
Reminds me of the memories that I thought I left behind
We've been apart for months, but it feels like days
I can still smell your hoodie and the scent of your ways

All yours, I belong to you
All yours, no one else will do
All yours, through thick and thin
All yours, love that's always been

Eating and drinking with our friends, sharing all our tales
You cook, I read, late-night sweets never fail
We danced, we laughed, felt like we were kids
You cared for me like one, my heart always skids

All yours, I belong to you
All yours, no one else will do
All yours, through thick and thin
All yours, love that's always been

You spoiled me like a princess, treated me like a queen
The small visits we had, made everything serene
The book with pictures of our trips, the midnights we shared

The old rusted key, the memories we bared

All yours, I belong to you
All yours, no one else will do
All yours, through thick and thin
All yours, love that's always been

18. Fragments of us

I'm walking down the street, lost in thought,
Wondering if you ever think of me, whether or not.
I pass by the places where we used to go,
The memories flooding back, fast and slow.

I can't help but wonder if you're doing okay,
If you found someone new to love, day by day.
But my heart still aches for the love we shared,
The one that felt so real, so true, so rare.

Oh, but darling, I still miss you so,
My heart can't let you go,
Every moment we had, every word we spoke,
Still echoes in my mind, like an unbroken oath.

I see your face in every crowd,
Hear your voice in every sound.
I try to push these thoughts away,
But they keep coming back, every single day.

I can't help but wonder if you're doing okay,
If you found someone new to love, day by day.
But my heart still aches for the love we shared,

The one that felt so real, so true, so rare.

Oh, but darling, I still miss you so,
My heart can't let you go,
Every moment we had, every word we spoke,
Still echoes in my mind, like an unbroken oath.

I know it's over, I know it's done,
But I can't help but feel like you're still the one.
Maybe someday we'll find our way back,
And the love we shared will never again lack.

Oh, but darling, I still miss you so,
My heart can't let you go,
Every moment we had, every word we spoke,
Still echoes in my mind, like an unbroken oath.

19. Heartstrings

We thought we had built a castle in the sand,
But the tide came in and washed it away, unplanned,
At 18, we dreamed of forevermore,
But at 28, we had to close that door.

With a knowing look, we both understood,
The moment had arrived as we thought it would,
No more hiding, no more delay,
It was time to face the truth and say.

The unnecessary fights and broken promises made
Hurtful comments and silence increasing like a cascade
Waiting and wanting for a long time, it's just a charade
All we have now is silence, our relationship in the shade

"This is too much!" I said with a sigh
Hurt and hurt only by how it's turned out, no need to lie
Although we gave all, still lost, no matter how we try
We're not wanting to meet, no more tears left to cry

As we part ways, the hurt is hard to conceal
Like a classic movie, our story had its appeal
But the credits have rolled, the ending has been sealed

"You had me at hello," the final dialogue we reveal.

20. Echoes of euphoria

In the stillness of the night,
I let go of what once was mine,
Releasing the grip of remembrances,
And embracing what the fate harbors in kind.

I let the winds of change carry me,
Far away from the distress and the hurt,
For it is in these instants of surrender,
That I find my true worth.

I am no longer held captive,
By the chains of what could have been,
For I have learned to treasure myself,
And to find solace within.

The road ahead may be rocky,
And the path may not be transparent,
But I trust in the journey of life,
And the lessons it brings tight.

Every ending senses like deja vu,
But I'm no longer shattered in two,
Step one and then step two, not blue,

Cherishing myself wholly, for a change of view.

End Note

Thank you for taking the time to read "The Ballad of Us." We hope these poems have touched you in a meaningful way and reminded you of the beauty and power of human connection.

As you reflect on these poems, I invite you to explore the many ways that love can manifest in our lives, from the quiet moments of tenderness to the fiery passion that ignites within us.

May these poems serve as a reminder that love is a flame that can never be extinguished, and that it burns bright within each of us, waiting to be kindled and shared with the world.

Thank you for joining me on this journey, and I hope these poems have inspired you to embrace the fullness of life and love.

Ingram Content Group UK Ltd.
Milton Keynes UK
UKHW011826170323
418736UK00004B/343